Custer and Other Poems by Ella Wheeler Wilcox

Poetry is a fascinating use of language. With almost a million words at its command it is not surprising that these Isles have produced some of the most beautiful, moving and descriptive verse through the centuries. In this series we look at the world through the eyes and minds of our most gifted poets to bring you a unique poetic guide to their lives.

Born on November 5th 1850 in Johnstown, Wisconsin, Ella Wheeler was the youngest of four children. She began to write as a child and by the time she graduated was already well known as a poet throughout Wisconsin.

Regarded more as a popular poet than a literary poet her most famous work 'Solitude' reflects on a train journey she made where giving comfort to a distressed fellow traveller she wrote how the others grief imposed itself for a time on her 'Laugh and the world laughs with you, Weep and you weep alone'. It was published in 1883 and was immensely popular.

The following year, 1884, she married Robert Wilcox. They lived for a time in New York before moving to Connecticut. Their only child, a son, died shortly after birth. It was around this time they developed an interest in spiritualism which for Ella would develop further into an interest in the occult. In later years this and works on positive thinking would occupy much of her writing.

On Robert's death in 1916 she spent months waiting for word from him from 'the other side' which never came.

In 1918 she published her autobiography The Worlds And I.

Ella died of cancer on October 30th, 1919.

Preface.
"Let such teach others, who themselves excel,
And censure freely who have written well."
POPE.

INDEX OF POEMS

The World's Need

So many gods, so many creeds,
So many paths that wind and wind,
While just the art of being kind,
Is all the sad world needs.

High Noon

Time's finger on the dial of my life
Points to high noon! and yet the half-spent day
Leaves less than half remaining, for the dark,
Bleak shadows of the grave engulf the end.

To those who burn the candle to the stick,
The sputtering socket yields but little light.
Long life is sadder than an early death.
We cannot count on raveled threads of age
Whereof to weave a fabric. We must use
The warp and woof the ready present yields
And toil while daylight lasts. When I bethink
How brief the past, the future still more brief,
Calls on to action, action! Not for me
Is time for retrospection or for dreams,
Not time for self-laudation or remorse.
Have I done nobly? Then I must not let
Dead yesterday unborn to-morrow shame.
Have I done wrong? Well, let the bitter taste
Of fruit that turned to ashes on my lip
Be my reminder in temptation's hour,
And keep me silent when I would condemn.
Sometimes it takes the acid of a sin
To cleanse the clouded windows of our souls
So pity may shine through them.

Looking back,
My faults and errors seem like stepping-stones

That led the way to knowledge of the truth
And made me value virtue; sorrows shine
In rainbow colors o'er the gulf of years,
Where lie forgotten pleasures.

Looking forth,
Out to the western sky still bright with noon,
I feel well spurred and booted for the strife
That ends not till Nirvana is attained.

Battling with fate, with men and with myself,
Up the steep summit of my life's forenoon,
Three things I learned, three things of precious worth
To guide and help me down the western slope.
I have learned how to pray, and toil, and save.
To pray for courage to receive what comes,
Knowing what comes to be divinely sent.
To toil for universal good, since thus
And only thus can good come unto me.
To save, by giving whatsoe'er I have
To those who have not, this alone is gain.

Transformation
She waited in a rose-hued room;
A wanton-hearted creature she,
But beautiful and bright to see
As some great orchid just in bloom.

Upon wide cushions stretched at ease
She lolled in garments filmy fine,
Which but enhanced each rounded line;
A living picture, framed to please.

A bold electric eye of light
Leered through its ruddy screen of lace
And feasted on her form and face
As some wine-crimsoned roué might.

From wall and niche, nude nymph beguiled
Fair goddesses of world-wide fame,
But Psyche's self was put to shame
By one who from the cushions smiled.

Exotic blossoms from a vase
Their sweet narcotic breath exhaled;
The lights, the objects round her paled

She lost the sense of time and place.

She seemed to float upon the air,
Untrammeled, unrestricted, free;
And rising from a vapory sea
She saw a form divinely fair.

A beauteous being in whose face
Shone all things sweet and true and good.
The innocence of maidenhood,
The motherhood of all the race.

The warmth which comes from heavenly fire,
The strength which leads the weaker man
To climb to God's Eternal plan
And conquer and control desire.

She shook as with a mighty awe,
For, gazing on this shape which stood
Embodying all true womanhood,
She knew it was herself she saw.

She woke as from a dream. But when
The laughing lover, light and bold
Came with his talk of wine and gold
He gazed, grew silent, gazed again;

Then turned abashed from those calm eyes
Where lurked no more the lure to sin.
Her higher self had entered in,
Her path led now to Paradise.

Thought-Magnets

With each strong thought, with every earnest longing
For aught thou deemest needful to thy soul,
Invisible vast forces are set thronging
Between thee and that goal.

'Tis only when some hidden weakness alters
And changes thy desire, or makes it less,
That this mysterious army ever falters
Or stops short of success.

Thought is a magnet; and the longed-for pleasure
Or boon, or aim, or object, is the steel;
And its attainment hangs but on the measure

Of what thy soul can feel.

Smiles

Smile a little, smile a little,
As you go along,
Not alone when life is pleasant,
But when things go wrong.
Care delights to see you frowning,
Loves to hear you sigh;
Turn a smiling face upon her,
Quick the dame will fly.

Smile a little, smile a little,
All along the road;
Every life must have its burden,
Every heart its load.
Why sit down in gloom and darkness,
With your grief to sup?
As you drink Fate's bitter tonic,
Smile across the cup.

Smile upon the troubled pilgrims
Whom you pass and meet;
Frowns are thorns, and smiles are blossoms
Oft for weary feet.

Do not make the way seem harder
By a sullen face,
Smile a little, smile a little,
Brighten up the place.

Smile upon your undone labor;
Not for one who grieves
O'er his task, waits wealth or glory;
He who smiles achieves.
Though you meet with loss and sorrow
In the passing years,
Smile a little, smile a little,
Even through your tears.

The Undiscovered Country

Man has explored all countries and all lands,
And made his own the secrets of each clime.
Now, ere the world has fully reached its prime,
The oval earth lies compassed with steel bands;

The seas are slaves to ships that touch all strands,
And even the haughty elements sublime
And bold, yield him their secrets for all time,
And speed like lackeys forth at his commands.

Still, though he search from shore to distant shore,
And no strange realms, no unlocated plains
Are left for his attainment and control,
Yet is there one more kingdom to explore.
Go, know thyself, O man! there yet remains
The undiscovered country of thy soul!

The Universal Route

As we journey along, with a laugh and a song,
We see, on youth's flower-decked slope,
Like a beacon of light, shining fair on the sight,
The beautiful Station of Hope.

But the wheels of old Time roll along as we climb,
And our youth speeds away on the years;
And with hearts that are numb with life's sorrows we come
To the mist-covered Station of Tears.

Still onward we pass, where the milestones, alas!
Are the tombs of our dead, to the West,
Where glitters and gleams, in the dying sunbeams,
The sweet, silent Station of Rest.

All rest is but change, and no grave can estrange
The soul from its Parent above;
And, scorning the rod, it soars back to its God,
To the limitless City of Love.

Earthly Pride

How baseless is the mightiest earthly pride,
The diamond is but charcoal purified,
The lordliest pearl that decks a monarch's breast
Is but an insect's sepulchre at best.

Unanswered Prayers

Like some school master, kind in being stern,
Who hears the children crying o'er their slates
And calling, "Help me master!" yet helps not,
Since in his silence and refusal lies

Their self-development, so God abides
Unheeding many prayers. He is not deaf
To any cry sent up from earnest hearts,
He hears and strengthens when He must deny.
He sees us weeping over life's hard sums
But should He give the key and dry our tears
What would it profit us when school were done
And not one lesson mastered?

What a world
Were this if all our prayers were answered. Not
In famed Pandora's box were such vast ills
As lie in human hearts. Should our desires
Voiced one by one in prayer ascend to God
And come back as events shaped to our wish
What chaos would result!

In my fierce youth
I sighed out breath enough to move a fleet
Voicing wild prayers to heaven for fancied boons
Which were denied; and that denial bends
My knee to prayers of gratitude each day
Of my maturer years. Yet from those prayers
I rose alway regirded for the strife
And conscious of new strength. Pray on, sad heart,
That which thou pleadest for may not be given
But in the lofty altitude where souls
Who supplicate God's grace are lifted there
Thou shalt find help to bear thy daily lot
Which is not elsewhere found.

Thanksgiving
We walk on starry fields of white
And do not see the daisies;
For blessings common in our sight
We rarely offer praises.
We sigh for some supreme delight
To crown our lives with splendor,
And quite ignore our daily store
Of pleasures sweet and tender.

Our cares are bold and push their way
Upon our thought and feeling.
They hang about us all the day,
Our time from pleasure stealing.
So unobtrusive many a joy

We pass by and forget it,
But worry strives to own our lives
And conquers if we let it.

There's not a day in all the year
But holds some hidden pleasure,
And looking back, joys oft appear
To brim the past's wide measure.
But blessings are like friends, I hold,
Who love and labor near us.
We ought to raise our notes of praise
While living hearts can hear us.

Full many a blessing wears the guise
Of worry or of trouble.
Farseeing is the soul and wise
Who knows the mask is double.
But he who has the faith and strength
To thank his God for sorrow
Has found a joy without alloy
To gladden every morrow,

We ought to make the moments notes
Of happy, glad Thanksgiving;
The hours and days a silent phrase
Of music we are living.
And so the theme should swell and grow
As weeks and months pass o'er us,
And rise sublime at this good time,
A grand Thanksgiving chorus.

A Maiden To Her Mirror
He said he loved me! Then he called my hair
Silk threads wherewith sly Cupid strings his bow,
My cheek a rose leaf fallen on new snow;
And swore my round, full throat would bring despair
To Venus or to Psyche.

Time and care
Will fade these locks; the merry god, I trow,
Uses no grizzled cords upon his bow.
How will it be when I, no longer fair,
Plead for his kiss with cheeks whence long ago
The early snowflakes melted quite away,
The rose leaf diedand in whose sallow clay
Lie the deep sunken tracks of life's gaunt crow?

When this full throat shall wattle fold on fold,
Like some ripe peach left drying on a wall,
Or like a spent accordion, when all
Its music has exhaled will love grow cold?

The Kettle

There's many a house of grandeur,
With turret, tower and dome,
That knows not peace or comfort,
And does not prove a home.
I do not ask for splendor
To crown my daily lot,
But this I ask a kitchen
Where the kettle's always hot.

If things are not all ship-shape,
I do not fume or fret,
A little clean disorder
Does not my nerves upset.
But one thing is essential,
Or seems so to my thought,
And that's a tidy kitchen
Where the kettle's always hot.

In my Aunt Hattie's household,
Though skies outside are drear,
Though times are dark and troubled,
You'll always find good cheer.
And in her quaint old kitchen
The very homiest spot
The kettle's always singing,
The water's always hot.

And if you have a headache,
Whate'er the hour may be,
There is no tedious waiting
To get your cup of tea.
I don't know how she does it
Some magic she has caught
For the kitchen's cool in summer,
Yet the kettle's always hot.

Oh, there's naught else so dreary
In household kingdom found
As a cold and sullen kettle

That does not make a sound.
And I think that love is lacking
In the hearts in such a spot,
Or the kettle would be singing
And the water would be hot.

Contrasts

I see the tall church steeples,
They reach so far, so far,
But the eyes of my heart see the world's great mart,
Where the starving people are.

I hear the church bells ringing
Their chimes on the morning air;
But my soul's sad ear is hurt to hear
The poor man's cry of despair.

Thicker and thicker the churches,
Nearer and nearer the sky
But alack for their creeds while the poor man's needs
Grow deeper as years roll by.

Thy Ship

Hadst thou a ship, in whose vast hold lay stored
The priceless riches of all climes and lands,
Say, wouldst thou let it float upon the seas
Unpiloted, of fickle winds the sport,
And of wild waves and hidden rocks the prey?

Thine is that ship; and in its depths concealed
Lies all the wealth of this vast universe
Yea, lies some part of God's omnipotence
The legacy divine of every soul.
Thy will, O man, thy will is that great ship,
And yet behold it drifting here and there
One moment lying motionless in port,
Then on high seas by sudden impulse flung,

Then drying on the sands, and yet again
Sent forth on idle quests to no-man's land
To carry nothing and to nothing bring;
Till worn and fretted by the aimless strife
And buffeted by vacillating winds
It founders on a rock, or springs aleak
With all its unused treasures in the hold.

Go save thy ship, thou sluggard; take the wheel
And steer to knowledge, glory and success.
Great mariners have made the pathway plain
For thee to follow; hold thou to the course
Of Concentration Channel, and all things
Shall come in answer to thy swerveless wish
As comes the needle to the magnet's call,
Or sunlight to the prisoned blade of grass
That yearns all winter for the kiss of spring.

The Tryst

Just when all hope had perished in my soul,
And balked desire made havoc with my mind,
My cruel Ladye suddenly grew kind,
And sent these gracious words upon a scroll:
"When knowing Night her dusky scarf has tied
Across the bold, intrusive eyes of day,
Come as a glad, triumphant lover may,
No longer fearing that he be denied."

I read her letter for the hundredth time,
And for the hundredth time my gladdened sight
Blurred with the rapture of my vast delight,
And swooned upon the page. I caught the chime
Of far off bells, and at each silver note
My heart on tiptoe pressed its eager ear
Against my breast; it was such joy to hear
The tolling of the hour of which she wrote.

The curious day still lingered in the skies
And watched me as I hastened to the tryst.
And back, beyond great clouds of amethyst,
I saw the Night's soft, reassuring eyes.
"Oh, Night," I cried, "dear Love's considerate friend,
Haste from the far, dim valleys of the west,
Rock the sad striving earth to quiet rest,
And bid the day's insistent vigil end."

Down brooding streets, and past the harbored ships
The Night's young handmaid, Twilight, walked with me.
A spent moon leaned inertly o'er the sea;
A few, pale, phantom stars were in eclipse.
There was the house, My Ladye's sea-girt bower
All draped in gloom, save for one taper's glow,
Which lit the path, where willing feet would go.

There was the house, and this the promised hour.

The tide was out; and from the sea's salt path
Rose amorous odors, filtering through the night
And stirring all the senses with delight;
Sweet perfumes left since Aphrodite's bath.
Back in the wooded copse, a whip-poor-will
Gave love's impassioned and impatient call.
On pebbled sands I heard the waves kiss fall,
And fall again, so hushed the hour and still.

Light was my knock upon the door, so light,
And yet the sound seemed rude. My pulses beat
So loud they drowned the coming of her feet
The arrow of her taper pierced the gloom
The portal closed behind me. She was there-
Love on her lips and yielding in her eyes
And but the sea to hear our vows and sighs.
She took my hand and led me up the stair.

Life
All in the dark we grope along,
And if we go amiss
We learn at least which path is wrong,
And there is gain in this.

We do not always win the race,
By only running right,
We have to tread the mountain's base
Before we reach its height.

The Christs alone no errors made;
So often had they trod
The paths that lead through light and shade,
They had become as God.

As Krishna, Buddha, Christ again,
They passed along the way,
And left those mighty truths which men
But dimly grasp to-day.

But he who loves himself the last
And knows the use of pain,
Though strewn with errors all his past,
He surely shall attain.

Some souls there are that needs must taste
Of wrong, ere choosing right;
We should not call those years a waste
Which led us to the light.

A Marine Etching

A yacht from its harbor ropes pulled free,
And leaped like a steed o'er the race track blue,
Then up behind her, the dust of the sea,
A gray fog drifted, and hid her from view.

The Duel

Oh many a duel the world has seen
That was bitter with hate, that was red with gore,
But I sing of a duel by far more cruel
Than ever by poet was sung before.
It was waged by night, yea by day and by night,
With never a pause or halt or rest,
And the curious spot where this battle was fought
Was the throbbing heart in a woman's breast.

There met two rivals in deadly strife,
And they fought for this woman so pale and proud.
One was a man in the prime of life,
And one was a corpse in a moldy shroud;
One wrapped in a sheet from his head to his feet,
The other one clothed in worldly fashion;
But a rival to dread is a man who is dead,
If he has been loved in life with passion.

The living lover he battled with sighs,
He strove for the woman with words that burned,
While stiff and stark lay the corpse in the dark,
And silently yearned and yearned and yearned.
One spoke of the rapture that life still held
For hearts that yielded to love's desire,
And one through the cold grave's earthy mold
Sent thoughts of a past that were fraught with fire.

The living lover seized hold of her hands
"You are mine," he cried, "and we will not part!"
But she felt the clutch of the dead man's touch
On the tense-drawn strings of her aching heart.
Yet the touch was of ice, and she shrank with fear
Oh! the hands of the dead are cold, so cold

And warm were the arms that waited near
To gather her close in their clinging fold.

And warm was the light in the living eyes,
But the eyes of the dead, how they stare and stare!
With sudden surrender she turned to the tender
And passionate lover who wooed her there.
Farewell to sorrow, hail, sweet to-morrow!
The battle was over, the duel was done.
They swooned in the blisses of love's fond kisses,
And the dead man stared on in the dark alone.

"Love Thyself Last"

Love thyself last. Look near, behold thy duty
To those who walk beside thee down life's road;
Make glad their days by little acts of beauty,
And help them bear the burden of earth's load.

Love thyself last. Look far and find the stranger,
Who staggers 'neath his sin and his despair;
Go lend a hand, and lead him out of danger,
To hights where he may see the world is fair.

Love thyself last. The vastnesses above thee
Are filled with Spirit Forces, strong and pure.
And fervently, these faithful friends shall love thee:
Keep thou thy watch o'er others and endure.

Love thyself last; and oh, such joy shall thrill thee,
As never yet to selfish souls was given.
Whate'er thy lot, a perfect peace will fill thee,
And earth shall seem the ante-room of Heaven.

Love thyself last, and them shall grow in spirit
To see, to hear, to know, and understand.
The message of the stars, lo, thou shall hear it,
And all God's joys shall be at thy command.

Christmas Fancies

When Christmas bells are swinging above the fields of snow,
We hear sweet voices ringing from lands of long ago.
And etched on vacant places,
Are half forgotten faces
Of friends we used to cherish, and loves we used to know
When Christmas bells are swinging above the fields of snow.

Uprising from the ocean of the present surging near,
We see, with strange emotion that is not free from fear,
That continent Elysian
Long vanished from our vision,
Youth's lovely lost Atlantis, so mourned for and so dear,
Uprising from the ocean of the present surging near.

When gloomy gray Decembers are roused to Christmas mirth,
The dullest life remembers there once was joy on earth,
And draws from youth's recesses
Some memory it possesses,
And, gazing through the lens of time, exaggerates its worth,
When gloomy gray December is roused to Christmas mirth.

When hanging up the holly or mistletoe, I wis
Each heart recalls some folly that lit the world with bliss.
Not all the seers and sages
With wisdom of the ages
Can give the mind such pleasure as memories of that kiss
When hanging up the holly or mistletoe, I wis.

For life was made for loving, and love alone repays,
As passing years are proving for all of Time's sad ways.
There lies a sting in pleasure,
And fame gives shallow measure,
And wealth is but a phantom that mocks the restless days,
For life was made for loving, and only loving pays.

When Christmas bells are pelting the air with silver chimes,
And silences are melting to soft, melodious rhymes,
Let Love, the world's beginning,
End fear and hate and sinning;
Let Love, the God Eternal, be worshiped in all climes
When Christmas bells are pelting the air with silver chimes.

The River
I am a river flowing from God's sea
Through devious ways. He mapped my course for me;
I cannot change it; mine alone the toil
To keep the waters free from grime and soil.
The winding river ends where it began;
And when my life has compassed its brief span
I must return to that mysterious source.
So let me gather daily on my course
The perfume from the blossoms as I pass,

Balm from the pines, and healing from the grass,
And carry down my current as I go
Not common stones but precious gems to show;
And tears (the holy water from sad eyes)
Back to God's sea, from which all rivers rise
Let me convey, not blood from wounded hearts,
Nor poison which the upas tree imparts.
When over flowery vales I leap with joy,
Let me not devastate them, nor destroy,
But rather leave them fairer to the sight;
Mine be the lot to comfort and delight.
And if down awful chasms I needs must leap
Let me not murmur at my lot, but sweep
On bravely to the end without one fear,
Knowing that He who planned my ways stands near.
Love sent me forth, to Love I go again,
For Love is all, and over all. Amen.

Sorry

There is much that makes me sorry as I journey down life's way,
And I seem to see more pathos in poor human lives each day.
I'm sorry for the strong brave men, who shield the weak from harm,
But who, in their own troubled hours find no protecting arm.

I am sorry for the victors who have reached success, to stand
As targets for the arrows shot by envious failure's hand.
I'm sorry for the generous hearts who freely shared their wine,
But drink alone the gall of tears in fortune's drear decline.

I'm sorry for the souls who build their own fame's funeral pyre,
Derided by the scornful throng like ice deriding fire.
I'm sorry for the conquering ones who know not sin's defeat,
But daily tread down fierce desire 'neath scorched and bleeding feet.

I'm sorry for the anguished hearts that break with passion's strain,
But I'm sorrier for the poor starved souls that never knew love's pain.
Who hunger on through barren years not tasting joys they crave,
For sadder far is such a lot than weeping o'er a grave.

I'm sorry for the souls that come unwelcomed into birth,
I'm sorry for the unloved old who cumber up the earth.
I'm sorry for the suffering poor in life's great maelstrom hurled,
In truth I'm sorry for them all who make this aching world.

But underneath whate'er seems sad and is not understood,
I know there lies hid from our sight a mighty germ of good.

And this belief stands firm by me, my sermon, motto, text
The sorriest things in this life will seem grandest in the next.

The Old Wooden Cradle

Good-bye to the cradle, the dear wooden cradle
The rude hand of Progress has thrust it aside.
No more to its motion o'er sleep's fairy ocean,
Our play-weary wayfarers peacefully glide.

No more by the rhythm of slow-moving rocker,
Their sweet dreamy fancies are fostered and fed;
No more to low singing the cradle goes swinging
The child of this era is put into bed.

Good-bye to the cradle, the dear wooden cradle,
It lent to the twilight a strange, subtle charm;
When bees left the clover, when play-time was over,
How safe seemed this shelter from danger or harm.

How soft seemed the pillow, how distant the ceiling,
How weird were the voices that whispered around,
What dreams would come flocking, as rocking and rocking,
We floated away into slumber profound.

Good-bye to the cradle, the old wooden cradle,
The babe of to-day does not know it by sight.
When day leaves the border, with system and order,
The child goes to bed and we put out the light.

I bow to Progression and ask no concession,
Though strewn be her pathway with wrecks of the past;
So off with old lumber, that sweet ark of slumber,
The old wooden cradle, is ruthlessly cast.

Ambition's Trail

If all the end of this continuous striving
Were simply to attain,
How poor would seem the planning and contriving
The endless urging and the hurried driving
Of body, heart and brain!

But ever in the wake of true achieving,
There shines this glowing trail
Some other soul will be spurred on, conceiving,
New strength and hope, in its own power believing,

Because thou didst not fail.

Not thine alone the glory, nor the sorrow,
If thou doth miss the goal,
Undreamed of lives in many a far to-morrow
From thee their weakness or their force shall borrow
On, on, ambitious soul.

The Traveled Man

Sometimes I wish the railroads all were torn out,
The ships all sunk among the coral strands.
I am so very weary, yea so worn out,
With tales of those who visit foreign lands.

When asked to dine, to meet these traveled people,
My soup seems brewed from cemetery bones.
The fish grows cold on some cathedral steeple,
I miss two courses while I stare at thrones.

I'm forced to leave my salad quite untasted,
Some musty, moldy temple to explore.
The ices, fruit and coffee all are wasted
While into realms of ancient art I soar.

I'd rather take my chance of life and reason,
If in a den of roaring lions hurled
Than for a single year, ay, for one season,
To dwell with folks who'd traveled round the world.

So patronizing are they, so oppressive,
With pity for the ones who stay at home,
So mighty is their knowledge so aggressive,
I ofttimes wish they had not ceased to roam.

They loathe the new, they quite detest the present;
They revel in a pre-Columbian morn;
Just dare to say America is pleasant,
And die beneath the glances of their scorn.

They are increasing at a rate alarming,
Go where I will, the traveled man is there.
And now I think that rustic wholly charming
Who has not strayed beyond his meadows fair.

Uncontrolled

The mighty forces of mysterious space
Are one by one subdued by lordly man.
The awful lightning that for eons ran
Their devastating and untrammeled race,
Now bear his messages from place to place
Like carrier doves. The winds lead on his van;
The lawless elements no longer can
Resist his strength, but yield with sullen grace.

His bold feet scaling heights before untrod,
Light, darkness, air and water, heat and cold
He bids go forth and bring him power and pelf.
And yet though ruler, king and demi-god
He walks with his fierce passions uncontrolled
The conquerer of all things save himself.

The Tulip Bed At Greeley Square
You know that oasis, fresh and fair
In the city desert, as Greeley square?

That bright triangle of scented bloom
That lies surrounded by grime and gloom?

Right in the breast of the seething town
Like a gleaming gem or a wanton's gown?

Ah, wonderful things that tulip bed
Unto my listening soul has said.

Over the rattle and roar of the street
I hear a chorus of voices sweet,

Day and night, when I pass that way,
And these are the things the voices say:

"Here, in the heart of the foolish strife,
We live a simple and natural life.

"Here, in the midst of the clash and din,
We know what it is to be calm within.

"Here, environed by sin and shame,
We do what we can with our pure white flame.

"We do what we can with our bloom and grace,
To make the city a fairer place.

"It is well to be good though the world is vile,
And so through the dust and the smoke we smile,

"We are but atoms in chaos tossed,
Yet never a purpose for truth was lost."

Ah, many a sermon is uttered there
By the bed of blossoms in Greeley square.

And he who listens and hears aright,
Is better equipped for the world's hard fight.

Will
You will be what you will to be;
Let failure find its false content
In that poor word "environment,"
But spirit scorns it, and is free,

It masters time, it conquers space,
It cows that boastful trickster Chance,
And bids the tyrant Circumstance
Uncrown and fill a servant's place.

The human Will, that force unseen,
The offspring of a deathless Soul,
Can hew the way to any goal,
Though walls of granite intervene.

Be not impatient in delay,
But wait as one who understands;
When spirit rises and commands,
The gods are ready to obey.

The river seeking for the sea
Confronts the dam and precipice,
Yet knows it cannot fail or miss;
You will be what you will to be!

To An Astrologer
Nay, seer, I do not doubt thy mystic lore,
Nor question that the tenor of my life,
Past, present and the future, is revealed
There in my horoscope. I do believe
That yon dead moon compels the haughty seas

To ebb and flow, and that my natal star
Stands like a stern-browed sentinel in space
And challenges events; nor lets one grief,
Or joy, or failure, or success, pass on
To mar or bless my earthly lot, until
It proves its Karmic right to come to me.

All this I grant, but more than this I know!
Before the solar systems were conceived,
When nothing was but the unnamable,
My spirit lived, an atom of the Cause.
Through countless ages and in many forms
It has existed, ere it entered in
This human frame to serve its little day
Upon the earth. The deathless Me of me,
The spark from that great all-creative fire
Is part of that eternal source called God,
And mightier than the universe.

Why, he
Who knows, and knowing, never once forgets
The pedigree divine of his own soul,
Can conquer, shape and govern destiny
And use vast space as 'twere a board for chess
With stars for pawns; can change his horoscope
To suit his will; turn failure to success,
And from preordained sorrows, harvest joy.

There is no puny planet, sun or moon,
Or zodiacal sign which can control
The God in us! If we bring that to bear
Upon events, we mold them to our wish,
'Tis when the infinite 'neath the finite gropes
That men are governed by their horoscopes.

The Tendril's Faith
Under the snow in the dark and the cold,
A pale little sprout was humming;
Sweetly it sang, 'neath the frozen mold,
Of the beautiful days that were coming.

"How foolish your songs," said a lump of clay,
"What is there, I ask, to prove them?
Just look at the walls between you and the day,
Now, have you the strength to move them?"

But under the ice and under the snow
The pale little sprout kept singing,
"I cannot tell how, but I know, I know,
I know what the days are bringing."

"Birds, and blossoms, and buzzing bees,
Blue, blue skies above me,
Bloom on the meadows and buds on the trees,
And the great glad sun to love me."

A pebble spoke next: "You are quite absurd."
It said, "with your song's insistence;
For I never saw a tree or a bird,
So of course there are none in existence."

"But I know, I know," the tendril cried,
In beautiful sweet unreason;
Till lo! from its prison, glorified,
It burst in the glad spring season.

The Times

The times are not degenerate. Man's faith
Mounts higher than of old. No crumbling creed
Can take from the immortal soul the need
Of that supreme Creator, God. The wraith
Of dead beliefs we cherished in our youth
Fades but to let us welcome new-born Truth.

Man may not worship at the ancient shrine
Prone on his face, in self-accusing scorn.
That night is past. He hails a fairer morn,
And knows himself a something all divine;
No humble worm whose heritage is sin,
But, born of God, he feels the Christ within.

Not loud his prayers, as in the olden time,
But deep his reverence for that mighty force.
That occult working of the great all Source,
Which makes the present era so sublime.
Religion now means something high and broad,
And man stood never half so near to God.

The Question

Beside us in our seeking after pleasures,
Through all our restless striving after fame,

Through all our search for worldly gains and treasures,
There walketh one whom no man likes to name.
Silent he follows, veiled of form and feature,
Indifferent if we sorrow or rejoice,
Yet that day comes when every living creature
Must look upon his face and hear his voice.

When that day comes to you, and Death, unmasking,
Shall bar your path, and say, "Behold the end,"
What are the questions that he will be asking
About your past? Have you considered, friend?
I think he will not chide you for your sinning,
Nor for your creeds or dogmas will he care;
He will but ask, "From your life's first beginning
How many burdens have you helped to bear?"

Sorrow's Uses
The uses of sorrow I comprehend
Better and better at each year's end.

Deeper and deeper I seem to see
Why and wherefore it has to be.

Only after the dark, wet days
Do we fully rejoice in the sun's bright rays.

Sweeter the crust tastes after the fast
Than the sated gourmand's finest repast.

The faintest cheer sounds never amiss
To the actor who once has heard a hiss.

To one who the sadness of freedom knows,
Light seem the fetters love may impose.

And he who has dwelt with his heart alone,
Hears all the music in friendship's tone.

So better and better I comprehend,
How sorrow ever would be our friend.

If
Twixt what thou art, and what thou wouldst be, let
No "If" arise on which to lay the blame.
Man makes a mountain of that puny word,

But, like a blade of grass before the scythe,
It falls and withers when a human will,
Stirred by creative force, sweeps toward its aim.

Thou wilt be what thou couldst be. Circumstance
Is but the toy of genius. When a soul
Burns with a god-like purpose to achieve,
All obstacles between it and its goal
Must vanish as the dew before the sun.

"If" is the motto of the dilettante
And idle dreamer; 'tis the poor excuse
Of mediocrity. The truly great
Know not the word, or know it but to scorn,
Else had Joan of Arc a peasant died,
Uncrowned by glory and by men unsung.

Which Are You?

There are two kinds of people on earth to-day;
Just two kinds of people, no more, I say.

Not the sinner and the saint, for it's well understood,
The good are half bad and the bad are half good.

Not the rich and the poor, for to rate a man's wealth,
You must first know the state of his conscience and health.

Not the humble and proud, for in life's little span,
Who puts on vain airs, is not counted a man.

Not the happy and sad, for the swift flying years
Bring each man his laughter and each man his tears.

No; the two kinds of people on earth I mean,
Are the people who lift, and the people who lean.

Wherever you go, you will find the earth's masses,
Are always divided in just these two classes.

And oddly enough, you will find too, I ween,
There's only one lifter to twenty who lean.

In which class are you? Are you easing the load,
Of overtaxed lifters, who toil down the road?

Or are you a leaner, who lets others share

Your portion of labor, and worry and care?

The Creed To Be

Our thoughts are molding unmade spheres,
And, like a blessing or a curse,
They thunder down the formless years,
And ring throughout the universe.

We build our futures, by the shape
Of our desires, and not by acts.
There is no pathway of escape;
No priest-made creeds can alter facts.

Salvation is not begged or bought;
Too long this selfish hope sufficed;
Too long man reeked with lawless thought,
And leaned upon a tortured Christ.

Like shriveled leaves, these worn out creeds
Are dropping from Religion's tree;
The world begins to know its needs,
And souls are crying to be free.

Free from the load of fear and grief,
Man fashioned in an ignorant age;
Free from the ache of unbelief
He fled to in rebellious rage.

No church can bind him to the things
That fed the first crude souls, evolved;
For, mounting up on daring wings,
He questions mysteries all unsolved.

Above the chant of priests, above
The blatant voice of braying doubt,
He hears the still, small voice of Love,
Which sends its simple message out.

And clearer, sweeter, day by day,
Its mandate echoes from the skies,
"Go roll the stone of self away,
And let the Christ within thee rise."

Music In The Flat

When Tom and I were married, we took a little flat;

I had a taste for singing and playing and all that.
And Tom, who loved to hear me, said he hoped I would not stop
All practice, like so many wives who let their music drop.
So I resolved to set apart an hour or two each day
To keeping vocal chords and hands in trim to sing and play.

The second morning I had been for half an hour or more
At work on Haydn's masses, when a tap came at my door.
A nurse who wore a dainty cap and apron, and a smile,
Ran down to ask if I would cease my music for awhile.
The lady in the flat above was very ill, she said,
And the sound of my piano was distracting to her head.

A fortnight's exercises lost, ere I began them, when,
The following morning at my door, there came that tap again;
A woman with an anguished face implored me to forego
My music for some days to come a man was dead below.
I shut down my piano till the corpse had left the house,
And spoke to Tom in whispers and was quiet as a mouse.

A week of labor limbered up my stiffened hand and voice,
I stole an extra hour from sleep, to practice and rejoice;
When, ting-a-ling, the door-bell rang a discord in my trill
The baby in the flat across was very, very ill.
For ten long days that infant's life was hanging by a thread,
And all that time my instrument was silent as the dead.

So pain and death and sickness came in one perpetual row,
When babies were not born above, then tenants died below.
The funeral over underneath, someone fell ill on top,
And begged me, for the love of God, to let my music drop.
When trouble went not up or down, it stalked across the hall,
And so in spite of my resolve, I do not play at all.

Inspiration
Not like a daring, bold, aggressive boy,
Is inspiration, eager to pursue,
But rather like a maiden, fond, yet coy,
Who gives herself to him who best doth woo.

Once she may smile, or thrice, thy soul to fire,
In passing by, but when she turns her face,
Thou must persist and seek her with desire,
If thou wouldst win the favor of her grace.

And if, like some winged bird she cleaves the air,

And leaves thee spent and stricken on the earth,
Still must thou strive to follow even there,
That she may know thy valor and thy worth.

Then shall she come unveiling all her charms,
Giving thee joy for pain, and smiles for tears;
Then shalt thou clasp her with possessing arms,
The while she murmurs music in thine ears.

But ere her kiss has faded from thy cheek,
She shall flee from thee over hill and glade,
So must thou seek and ever seek and seek
For each new conquest of this phantom maid.

The Wish

Should some great angel say to me to-morrow,
"Thou must re-tread thy pathway from the start,
But God will grant, in pity, for thy sorrow,
Someone dear wish, the nearest to thy heart."

This were my wish! from my life's dim beginning
Let be what has been! wisdom planned the whole;
My want, my woe, my errors, and my sinning,
All, all were needed lessons for my soul.

Three Friends

Of all the blessings which my life has known,
I value most, and most praise God for three:
Want, Loneliness and Pain, those comrades true,

Who, masqueraded in the garb of foes
For many a year, and filled my heart with dread.
Yet fickle joys, like false, pretentious friends,
Have proved less worthy than this trio. First,

Want taught me labor, led me up the steep
And toilsome paths to hills of pure delight,
Trod only by the feet that know fatigue,
And yet press on until the heights appear.

Then loneliness and hunger of the heart
Sent me upreaching to the realms of space,
Till all the silences grew eloquent,
And all their loving forces hailed me friend.

Last, pain taught prayer! placed in my hand the staff
Of close communion with the over-soul,
That I might lean upon it till the end,
And find myself made strong for any strife.

And then these three who had pursued my steps
Like stern, relentless foes, year after year,
Unmasked, and turned their faces full on me,
And lo! they were divinely beautiful,
For through them shone the lustrous eyes of Love.

You Never Can Tell

You never can tell when you send a word,
Like an arrow shot from a bow
By an archer blind, be it cruel or kind,
Just where it may chance to go.
It may pierce the breast of your dearest friend.
Tipped with its poison or balm,
To a stranger's heart in life's great mart,
It may carry its pain or its calm

You never can tell when you do an act
Just what the result will be;
But with every deed you are sowing a seed,
Though the harvest you may not see.
Each kindly act is an acorn dropped
In God's productive soil
You may not know, but the tree shall grow,
With shelter for those who toil.

You never can tell what your thoughts will do,
In bringing you hate or love;
For thoughts are things, and their airy wings
Are swifter than carrier doves.
They follow the law of the universe
Each thing must create its kind,
And they speed o'er the track to bring you back
Whatever went out from your mind.

Here And Now

Here, in the heart of the world,
Here, in the noise and the din,
Here, where our spirits were hurled
To battle with sorrow and sin,
This is the place and the spot

For knowledge of infinite things;
This is the kingdom where Thought
Can conquer the prowess of kings.

Wait for no heavenly life,
Seek for no temple alone;
Here, in the midst of the strife,
Know what the sages have known.
See what the Perfect Ones saw
God in the depth of each soul,
God as the light and the law,
God as beginning and goal.

Earth is one chamber of Heaven,
Death is no grander than birth.
Joy in the life that was given,
Strive for perfection on earth.
Here, in the turmoil and roar,
Show what it is to be calm;
Show how the spirit can soar
And bring back its healing and balm.

Stand not aloof nor apart,
Plunge in the thick of the fight.
There in the street and the mart,
That is the place to do right.
Not in some cloister or cave,
Not in some kingdom above,
Here, on this side of the grave,
Here, should we labor and love.

Unconquered
However skilled and strong art thou, my foe,
However fierce is thy relentless hate
Though firm thy hand, and strong thy aim, and straight
Thy poisoned arrow leaves the bended bow,
To pierce the target of my heart, ah! know
I am the master yet of my own fate.
Thou canst not rob me of my best estate,
Though fortune, fame and friends, yea love shall go.

Not to the dust shall my true self be hurled;
Nor shall I meet thy worst assaults dismayed.
When all things in the balance are well weighed,
There is but one great danger in the world
Thou canst not force my soul to wish thee ill,

That is the only evil that can kill.

All That Love Asks

"All that I ask," says Love, "is just to stand
And gaze, unchided, deep in thy dear eyes;
For in their depths lies largest Paradise.
Yet, if perchance one pressure of thy hand
Be granted me, then joy I thought complete
Were still more sweet."

"All that I ask," says Love, "all that I ask,
Is just thy hand clasp. Could I brush thy cheek
As zephyrs brush a rose leaf, words are weak
To tell the bliss in which my soul would bask.
There is no language but would desecrate
A joy so great."

"All that I ask, is just one tender touch
Of that soft cheek. Thy pulsing palm in mine,
Thy dark eyes lifted in a trust divine
And those curled lips that tempt me overmuch
Turned where I may not seize the supreme bliss
Of one mad kiss.

"All that I ask," says Love, "of life, of death,
Or of high heaven itself, is just to stand,
Glance melting into glance, hand twined in hand,
The while I drink the nectar of thy breath,
In one sweet kiss, but one, of all thy store,
I ask no more."

"All that I ask" nay, self-deceiving Love,
Reverse thy phrase, so thus the words may fall,
In place of "all I ask," say, "I ask all,"
All that pertains to earth or soars above,
All that thou wert, art, will be, body, soul,
Love asks the whole.

Does It Pay

If one poor burdened toiler o'er life's road,
Who meets us by the way,
Goes on less conscious of his galling load,
Then life indeed, does pay.

If we can show one troubled heart the gain,

That lies alway in loss,
Why then, we too, are paid for all the pain
Of bearing life's hard cross.

If some despondent soul to hope is stirred,
Some sad lip made to smile,
By any act of ours, or any word,
Then, life has been worthwhile.

Sestina

I wandered o'er the vast green plains of youth,
And searched for Pleasure. On a distant height
Fame's silhouette stood sharp against the skies.
Beyond vast crowds that thronged a broad high-way
I caught the glimmer of a golden goal,
While from a blooming bower smiled siren Love.

Straight gazing in her eyes, I laughed at Love,
With all the haughty insolence of youth,
As past her bower I strode to seek my goal.
"Now will I climb to glory's dizzy height,"
I said, "for there above the common way
Doth pleasure dwell companioned by the skies."

But when I reached that summit near the skies,
So far from man I seemed, so far from Love
"Not here," I cried, "doth Pleasure find her way,"
Seen from the distant borderland of youth.
Fame smiles upon us from her sun-kissed height,
But frowns in shadows when we reach the goal.

Then were mine eyes fixed on that glittering goal,
Dear to all sense, sunk souls beneath the skies.
Gold tempts the artist from the lofty height,
Gold lures the maiden from the arms of Love,
Gold buys the fresh ingenuous heart of youth,
"And gold," I said, "will show me Pleasure's way."

But ah! the soil and discord of that way,
Where savage hordes rushed headlong to the goal,
Dead to the best impulses of their youth,
Blind to the azure beauty of the skies;
Dulled to the voice of conscience and of love,
They wandered far from Truth's eternal height.

Then Truth spoke to me from that noble height,

Saying: "Thou didst pass Pleasure on the way,
She with the yearning eyes so full of Love,
Whom thou disdained to seek for glory's goal."
Two blending paths beneath God's arching skies
Lead straight to Pleasure. Ah, blind heart of youth,
Not up fame's height, not toward the base god's goal,
Doth Pleasure make her way, but 'neath calm skies
Where Duty walks with Love in endless youth.

The Optimist

The fields were bleak and sodden. Not a wing
Or note enlivened the depressing wood,
A soiled and sullen, stubborn snowdrift stood
Beside the roadway. Winds came muttering
Of storms to be, and brought the chilly sting
Of icebergs in their breath. Stalled cattle mooed
Forth plaintive pleadings for the earth's green food.
No gleam, no hint of hope in anything.

The sky was blank and ashen, like the face
Of some poor wretch who drains life's cup too fast.
Yet, swaying to and fro, as if to fling
About chilled Nature its lithe arms of grace,
Smiling with promise in the wintry blast,
The optimistic Willow spoke of spring.

The Pessimist

The pessimistic locust, last to leaf,
Though all the world is glad, still talks of grief.

The Hammock's Complaint

Who thinks how desolate and strange
To me must seem the autumn's change,
When housed in attic or in chest,
A lonely and unwilling guest,
I lie through nights of bleak December,
And think in silence, and remember.

I think of hempen fields, where I
Once played with insects floating by,
And joyed alike in sun and rain,
Unconscious of approaching pain.
I dwell upon my later lot,
Where, swung in some secluded spot

Between two tried and trusted trees,
All summer long I wooed the breeze.
With song of bee and call of bird
And lover's secrets overheard,
And sight and scent of blooming flowers,
To fill the happy sunlight's hours.
When verdant fields grow bare and brown,
When forest leaves come raining down,
When frost has mated with the weather
And all the birds go south together,
When drying boats turn up their keels,
Who wonders how the hammock feels?

Life's Harmonies

Let no man pray that he know not sorrow,
Let no soul ask to be free from pain,
For the gall of to-day is the sweet of to-morrow,
And the moment's loss is the lifetime's gain.

Through want of a thing does its worth redouble,
Through hunger's pangs does the feast content,
And only the heart that has harbored trouble,
Can fully rejoice when joy is sent.

Let no man shrink from the bitter tonics
Of grief, and yearning, and need, and strife,
For the rarest chords in the soul's harmonies,
Are found in the minor strains of life.

Preaching vs. Practice

It is easy to sit in the sunshine
And talk to the man in the shade;
It is easy to float in a well-trimmed boat,
And point out the places to wade.

But once we pass into the shadows,
We murmur and fret and frown,
And, our length from the bank, we shout for a plank,
Or throw up our hands and go down.

It is easy to sit in your carriage,
And counsel the man on foot,
But get down and walk, and you'll change your talk,
As you feel the peg in your boot.

It is easy to tell the toiler
How best he can carry his pack,
But no one can rate a burden's weight
Until it has been on his back.

The up-curled mouth of pleasure,
Can prate of sorrow's worth,
But give it a sip, and a wryer lip,
Was never made on earth.

An Old Man To His Sleeping Young Bride

As when the old moon lighted by the tender
And radiant crescent of the new is seen,
And for a moment's space suggests the splendor
Of what in its full prime it once has been,
So on my waning years you cast the glory
Of youth and pleasure, for a little hour;
And life again seems like an unread story,
And joy and hope both stir me with their power.

Can blooming June be fond of bleak December?
I dare not wait to hear my heart reply.
I will forget the question and remember
Alone the priceless feast spread for mine eye,
That radiant hair that flows across the pillows,
Like shimmering sunbeams over drifts of snow;
Those heaving breasts, like undulating billows,
Whose dangers or delights but Love can know.

That crimson mouth from which sly Cupid borrowed
The pattern for his bow, nor asked consent;
That smooth, unruffled brow which has not sorrowed
All these are mine; should I not be content?
Yet are these treasures mine, or only lent me?
And who shall claim them when I pass away?
Oh, jealous Fate, to torture and torment me
With thoughts like these in my too fleeting day!

For while I gained the prize which all were seeking,
And won you with the ardor of my quest,
The bitter truth I know without your speaking
You only let me love you at the best.
E'en while I lean and count my riches over,
And view with gloating eyes your priceless charms,
I know somewhere there dwells the unnamed lover
Who yet shall clasp you, willing, in his arms.

And while my hands stray through your clustering tresses,
And while my lips are pressed upon your own,
This unseen lover waits for such caresses
As my poor hungering clay has never known,
And when some day, between you and your duty
A green grave lies, his love shall make you glad,
And you shall crown him with your splendid beauty
Ah, God! ah, God! 'tis this way men go mad!

I Am

I know not whence I came,
I know not whither I go;
But the fact stands clear that I am here
In this world of pleasure and woe.
And out of the mist and murk,
Another truth shines plain.
It is in my power each day and hour
To add to its joy or its pain.

I know that the earth exists,
It is none of my business why.
I cannot find out what it's all about,
I would but waste time to try.
My life is a brief, brief thing,
I am here for a little space.
And while I stay I would like, if I may,
To brighten and better the place.

The trouble, I think, with us all
Is the lack of a high conceit.
If each man thought he was sent to this spot
To make it a bit more sweet,
How soon we could gladden the world.
How easily right all wrong.
If nobody shirked, and each one worked
To help his fellows along.

Cease wondering why you came
Stop looking for faults and flaws.
Rise up to-day in your pride and say,
"I am part of the First Great Cause!
However full the world
There is room for an earnest man.
It had need of me or I would not be,
I am here to strengthen the plan."

Two Nights
(Suggested by the lives of Napoleon and Josephine.)

I.
One night was full of rapture and delight
Of reunited arms and swooning kisses,
And all the unnamed and unnumbered blisses
Which fond souls find in love of love at night.

Heart beat with heart, and each clung into each
With twining arms that did but loose their hold
To cling still closer; and fond glances told
These truths for which there is no uttered speech.

There was sweet laughter and endearing words,
Made broken by the kiss that could not wait,
And cooing sounds as of dear little birds
That in spring-time love and woo and mate.

And languid sighs that breathed of love's content
And all too soon this night of rapture went.

II.
One night was full of anguish and of pain,
Of nerveless arms and mockery of kisses;
And those caresses where one sick heart misses
The quick response the other cannot feign.

Hands idly clasped and unclasped, and lost hold,
And the averted eyes, that turned away,
And in whose depths no love nor longing lay,
The saddest of all truths too plainly told.

There was salt sorrow and the gall of tears,
Some useless words that ended in a moan,
And a dull dread of long unending years
When one must walk forever more alone.
Deep shuddering sighs told more than lips could say;
And the long night of sorrow wore away.

Preparation
We must not force events, but rather make
The heart soil ready for their coming, as
The earth spreads carpets for the feet of Spring,

Or, with the strengthening tonic of the frost,
Prepares for Winter. Should a July noon
Burst suddenly upon a frozen world
Small joy would follow, even tho' that world
Were longing for the Summer. Should the sting
Of sharp December pierce the heart of June,
What death and devastation would ensue!
All things are planned. The most majestic sphere
That whirls through space is governed and controlled
By supreme law, as is the blade of grass
Which through the bursting bosom of the earth
Creeps up to kiss the light. Poor puny man
Alone doth strive and battle with the Force
Which rules all lives and worlds, and he alone
Demands effect before producing cause.
How vain the hope! We cannot harvest joy
Until we sow the seed, and God alone
Knows when that seed has ripened. Oft we stand
And watch the ground with anxious brooding eyes
Complaining of the slow unfruitful yield,
Not knowing that the shadow of ourselves
Keeps off the sunlight and delays result.
Sometimes our fierce impatience of desire
Doth like a sultry May force tender shoots
Of half-formed pleasures and unshaped events
To ripen prematurely, and we reap
But disappointment; or we rot the germs
With briny tears ere they have time to grow.
While stars are born and mighty planets die
And hissing comets scorch the brow of space
The Universe keeps its eternal calm.
Through patient preparation, year on year,
The earth endures the travail of the Spring
And Winter's desolation. So our souls
In grand submission to a higher law
Should move serene through all the ills of life,
Believing them masked joys.

Custer

BOOK FIRST

I.
All valor died not on the plains of Troy.
Awake, my Muse, awake! be thine the joy
To sing of deeds as dauntless and as brave

As e'er lent luster to a warrior's grave.
Sing of that noble soldier, nobler man,
Dear to the heart of each American.
Sound forth his praise from sea to listening sea
Greece her Achilles claimed, immortal Custer, we.

II.

Intrepid are earth's heroes now as when
The gods came down to measure strength with men.
Let danger threaten or let duty call,
And self surrenders to the needs of all;
Incurs vast perils, or, to save those dear,
Embraces death without one sigh or tear.
Life's martyrs still the endless drama play
Though no great Homer lives to chant their worth to-day.

III.

And if he chanted, who would list his songs,
So hurried now the world's gold-seeking throngs?
And yet shall silence mantle mighty deeds?
Awake, dear Muse, and sing though no ear heeds!
Extol the triumphs, and bemoan the end
Of that true hero, lover, son and friend
Whose faithful heart in his last choice was shown
Death with the comrades dear, refusing flight alone.

IV.

He who was born for battle and for strife
Like some caged eagle frets in peaceful life;
So Custer fretted when detained afar
From scenes of stirring action and of war.
And as the captive eagle in delight,
When freedom offers, plumes himself for flight
And soars away to thunder clouds on high,
With palpitating wings and wild exultant cry.

V.

So lion-hearted Custer sprang to arms,
And gloried in the conflict's loud alarms.
But one dark shadow marred his bounding joy;
And then the soldier vanished, and the boy,
The tender son, clung close, with sobbing breath,
To her from whom each parting was new death;

That mother who like goddesses of old,
Gave to the mighty Mars, three warriors brave and bold,

VI.
Yet who, unlike those martial dames of yore,
Grew pale and shuddered at the sight of gore.
A fragile being, born to grace the hearth,
Untroubled by the conflicts of the earth.
Some gentle dove who reared young eaglets, might,
In watching those bold birdlings take their flight,
Feel what that mother felt who saw her sons
Rush from her loving arms, to face death-dealing guns.

VII.
But ere thy lyre is strung to martial strains
Of wars which sent our hero o'er the plains,
To add the cypress to his laureled brow,
Be brave, my Muse, and darker truths avow.
Let Justice ask a preface to thy songs,
Before the Indian's crimes declare his wrongs;
Before effects, wherein all horrors blend,
Declare the shameful cause, precursor of the end.

VIII.
When first this soil the great Columbus trod,
He was less like the image of his God
Than those ingenuous souls, unspoiled by art,
Who lived so near to Mother Nature's heart;
Those simple children of the wood and wave,
As frank as trusting, and as true as brave;
Savage they were, when on some hostile raid
(For where is he so high, whom war does not degrade?)

IX.
But dark deceit and falsehood's shameless shame
They had not learned, until the white man came.
He taught them, too, the lurking devil's joy
In liquid lies, that lure but to destroy.
With wily words, as false as they were sweet,
He spread his snares for unsuspecting feet;
Paid truth with guile, and trampled in the dust
Their gentle childlike faith and unaffected trust.

X.
And for the sport of idle kings and knaves
Of Nature's greater noblemen, made slaves.
Alas, the hour, when the wronged Indian knows
His seeming benefactors are but foes.
His kinsmen kidnapped and his lands possessed,
The demon woke in that untutored breast.
Four hundred years have rolled upon their way
The ruthless demon rules the red man to this day.

XI.
If, in the morning of success, that grand
Invincible discoverer of our land
Had made no lodge or wigwam desolate
To carry trophies to the proud and great;
If on our history's page there were no blot
Left by the cruel rapine of Cabot,
Of Verrazin, and Hudson, dare we claim
The Indian of the plains, to day had been the same?

XII.
For in this brief existence, not alone
Do our lives gather what our hands have sown,
But we reap, too, what others long ago
Sowed, careless of the harvests that might grow.
Thus hour by hour the humblest human souls
Inscribe in cipher on unending scrolls,
The history of nations yet to be;
Incite fierce bloody wars, to rage from sea to sea,

XIII.
Or pave the way to peace. There is no past,
So deathless are events results so vast.
And he who strives to make one act or hour
Stand separate and alone, needs first the power
To look upon the breaking wave and say,
"These drops were bosomed by a cloud to-day,
And those from far mid-ocean's crest were sent."
So future, present, past, in one wide sea are blent.

BOOK SECOND

I.

Oh, for the power to call to aid, of mine
Own humble Muse, the famed and sacred nine.
Then might she fitly sing, and only then,
Of those intrepid and unflinching men
Who knew no homes save ever moving tents,
And who 'twixt fierce unfriendly elements
And wild barbarians warred. Yet unfraid,
Since love impels thy strains, sing, sing, my modest maid.

II.

Relate how Custer in midwinter sought
Far Washita's cold shores; tell why he fought
With savage nomads fortressed in deep snows.
Woman, thou source of half the sad world's woes
And all its joys, what sanguinary strife
Has vexed the earth and made contention rife
Because of thee! For, hidden in man's heart,
Ay, in his very soul, of his true self a part,

III.

The natural impulse and the wish belongs
To win thy favor and redress thy wrongs.
Alas! for woman, and for man, alas!
If that dread hour should ever come to pass,
When, through her new-born passion for control,
She drives that beauteous impulse from his soul.
What were her vaunted independence worth
If to obtain she sells her sweetest rights of birth?

IV.

God formed fair woman for her true estate
Man's tender comrade, and his equal mate,
Not his competitor in toil and trade.
While coarser man, with greater strength was made
To fight her battles and her rights protect.
Ay! to protect the rights of earth's elect
(The virgin maiden and the spotless wife)
From immemorial time has man laid down his life.

V.

And now brave Custer's valiant army pressed
Across the dangerous desert of the West,

To rescue fair white captives from the hands
Of brutal Cheyenne and Comanche bands,
On Washita's bleak banks. Nine hundred strong
It moved its slow determined way along,
Past frontier homes left dark and desolate
By the wild Indians' fierce and unrelenting hate;

VI.
Past forts where ranchmen, strong of heart and bold,
Wept now like orphaned children as they told,
With quivering muscles and with anguished breath,
Of captured wives, whose fate was worse than death;
Past naked bodies whose disfiguring wounds
Spoke of the hellish hate of human hounds;
Past bleaching skeleton and rifled grave,
On pressed th' avenging host, to rescue and to save.

VII.
Uncertain Nature, like a fickle friend,
(Worse than the foe on whom we may depend)
Turned on these dauntless souls a brow of wrath
And hurled her icy jav'lins in their path.
With treacherous quicksands, and with storms that blight,
Entrapped their footsteps and confused their sight.
"Yet on," urged Custer, "on at any cost,
No hour is there to waste, no moment to be lost."

VIII.
Determined, silent, on they rode, and on,
Like fabled Centaurs, men and steeds seemed one.
No bugle echoed and no voice spoke near,
Lest on some lurking Indian's list'ning ear
The sound might fall. Through swift descending snow
The stealthy guides crept, tracing out the foe;
No fire was lighted, and no halt was made
From haggard gray-lipped dawn till night lent friendly shade.

IX.
Then, by the shelt'ring river's bank at last,
The weary warriors paused for their repast.
A couch of ice and falling snows for spread
Made many a suffering soldier's chilling bed.
They slept to dream of glory and delight,

While the pale fingers of the pitying night
Wove ghostly winding sheets for that doomed score
Who, ere another eve, should sleep to wake no more.

X.
But those who slept not, saw with startled eyes
Far off, athwart dim unprotecting skies,
Ascending slowly with majestic grace,
A lustrous rocket, rising out of space.
"Behold the signal of the foe," cried one,
The field is lost before the strife's begun.
Yet no! for see! yon rays spread near and far;
It is the day's first smile, the radiant morning star.

XI.
The long hours counting till the daylight broke,
In whispered words the restless warriors spoke.
They talked of battles, but they thought of home
(For hearts are faithful though the feet may roam).
Brave Hamilton, all eager for the strife,
Mused o'er that two-fold mystery, death and life;
"And when I die," quoth he, "mine be the part
To fall upon the field, a bullet in my heart."

XII.
At break of dawn the scouts crept in to say
The foe was camped a rifle shot away.
The baying of a dog, an infant's cry
Pierced through the air; sleep fled from every eye.
To horse! to arms! the dead demand the dead!
Let the grand charge upon the lodge be led!
Let the Mosaic law, life for a life
Pay the long standing debt of blood. War to the knife!

XIII.
So spake each heart in that unholy rage
Which fires the brain, when war the thoughts engage.
War, hideous war, appealing to the worst
In complex man, and waking that wild thirst
For human blood which blood alone can slake.
Yet for their country's safety, and the sake
Of tortured captives moaning in alarm
The Indian must be made to fear the law's strong arm.

XIV.

A noble vengeance burned in Custer's breast,
But, as he led his army to the crest,
Above the wigwams, ready for the charge
He felt the heart within him, swelling large
With human pity, as an infant's wail
Shrilled once again above the wintry gale.
Then hosts of murdered children seemed to rise;
And shame his halting thought with sad accusing eyes,

XV.

And urge him on to action. Stern of brow
The just avenger, and the General now,
He gives the silent signal to the band
Which, all impatient, waits for his command.
Cold lips to colder metal press; the air
Echoes those merry strains which mean despair
For sleeping chieftain and for toiling squaw,
But joy to those stern hearts which glory in the law

XVI.

Of murder paying murder's awful debt.
And now four squadrons in one charge are met.
From east and west, from north and south they come,
At call of bugle and at roll of drum.
Their rifles rain hot hail upon the foe,
Who flee from danger in death's jaws to go.
The Indians fight like maddened bulls at bay,
And dying shriek and groan, wound the young ear of day.

XVII.

A pallid captive and a white-browed boy
Add to the tumult piercing cries of joy,
As forth they fly, with high hope animate.
A hideous squaw pursues them with her hate;
Her knife descends with sickening force and sound;
Their bloody entrails stain the snow-clad ground.
She shouts with glee, then yells with rage and falls
Dead by her victims' side, pierced by avenging balls.

XVIII.

Now war runs riot, carnage reigns supreme.
All thoughts of mercy fade from Custer's scheme.
Inhuman methods for inhuman foes,
Who feed on horrors and exult in woes.
To conquer and subdue alone remains
In dealing with the red man on the plains.
The breast that knows no conscience yields to fear,
Strike! let the Indian meet his master now and here.

XIX.

With thoughts like these was Custer's mind engaged.
The gentlest are the sternest when enraged.
All felt the swift contagion of his ire,
For he was one who could arouse and fire
The coldest heart, so ardent was his own.
His fearless eye, his calm intrepid tone,
Bespoke the leader, strong with conscious power,
Whom following friends will bless, while foes will curse and cower.

XX.

Again they charge! and now among the killed
Lies Hamilton, his wish so soon fulfilled,
Brave Elliott pursues across the field
The flying foe, his own young life to yield.
But like the leaves in some autumnal gale
The red men fall in Washita's wild vale.
Each painted face and black befeathered head
Still more repulsive seems with death's grim pallor wed.

XXI.

New forces gather on surrounding knolls,
And fierce and fiercer war's red river rolls.
With bright-hued pennants flying from each lance
The gayly costumed Kiowas advance.
And bold Comanches (Bedouins of the land)
Infuse fresh spirit in the Cheyenne band.
While from the ambush of some dark ravine
Flash arrows aimed by hands, unerring and unseen.

XXIII.

The hours advance; the storm clouds roll away;
Still furious and more furious grows the fray.
The yellow sun makes ghastlier still the sight

Of painted corpses, staring in its light.
No longer slaves, but comrades of their griefs,
The squaws augment the forces of their chiefs.
They chant weird dirges in a minor key,
While from the narrow door of wigwam and tepee

XXIV.
Cold glittering eyes above cold glittering steel
Their deadly purpose and their hate reveal.
The click of pistols and the crack of guns
Proclaim war's daughters dangerous as her sons.
She who would wield the soldier's sword and lance
Must be prepared to take the soldier's chance.
She who would shoot must serve as target, too;
The battle-frenzied men, infuriate now pursue.

XXV.
And blood of warrior, woman and papoose,
Flow free as waters when some dam breaks loose;
Consuming fire, the wanton friend of war
(Whom allies worship and whom foes abhor)
Now trails her crimson garments through the street,
And ruin marks the passing of her feet.
Full three-score lodges smoke upon the plain,
And all the vale is strewn with bodies of the slain.

XXVI.
And those who are not numbered with the dead
Before all-conquering Custer now are led.
To soothe their woes, and calm their fears he seeks;
An Osage guide interprets while he speaks.
The vanquished captives, humbled, cowed and spent
Read in the victor's eye his kind intent.
The modern victor is as kind as brave;
His captive is his guest, not his insulted slave.

XXVII.
Mahwissa, sister of the slaughtered chief
Of all the Cheyennes, listens; and her grief
Yields now to hope; and o'er her withered face
There flits the stealthy cunning of her race.
Then forth she steps, and thus begins to speak:
"To aid the fallen and support the weak

Is man's true province; and to ease the pain
Of those o'er whom it is his purpose now to reign.

XXVIII.
"Let the strong chief unite with theirs his life,
And take this black-eyed maiden for a wife."
Then, moving with an air of proud command,
She leads a dusky damsel by the hand,
And places her at wondering Custer's side,
Invoking choicest blessings on the bride
And all unwilling groom, who thus replies.
"Fair is the Indian maid, with bright bewildering eyes,

XXIX.
"But fairer still is one who, year on year,
Has borne man's burdens, conquered woman's fear;
And at my side rode mile on weary mile,
And faced all deaths, all dangers, with a smile,
Wise as Minerva, as Diana brave,
Is she whom generous gods in kindness gave
To share the hardships of my wandering life,
Companion, comrade, friend, my loved and loyal wife.

XXX.
"The white chief weds but one. Take back thy maid."
He ceased, and o'er Mahwissa's face a shade
Of mingled scorn and pity and surprise
Sweeps as she slow retreats, and thus replies:
"Rich is the pale-faced chief in battle fame,
But poor is he who but one wife may claim.
Wives are the red-skinned heroes' rightful spoil;
In war they prove his strength, in times of peace they toil."

XXXI.
But hark! The bugle echoes o'er the plains
And sounds again those merry Celtic strains
Which oft have called light feet to lilting dance,
But now they mean the order to advance.
Along the river's bank, beyond the hill
Two thousand foemen lodge, unconquered still.
Ere falls night's curtain on this bloody play,
The army must proceed, with feint of further fray.

XXXII.
The weary warriors mount their foam-flecked steeds,
With flags unfurled the dauntless host proceeds.
What though the foe outnumbers two to one?
Boldness achieves what strength oft leaves undone;
A daring mein will cause brute force to cower,
And courage is the secret source of power.
As Custer's column wheels upon their sight
The frightened red men yield the untried field by flight.

XXXIII.
Yet when these conquering heroes sink to rest,
Dissatisfaction gnaws the leader's breast,
For far away across vast seas of snows
Held prisoners still by hostile Arapahoes
And Cheyennes unsubdued, two captives wait.
On God and Custer hangs their future fate.
May the Great Spirit nerve the mortal's arm
To rescue suffering souls from worse than death's alarm.

XXXIV.
But ere they seek to rescue the oppressed,
The valiant dead, in state, are laid to rest.
Mourned Hamilton, the faithful and the brave,
Nine hundred comrades follow to the grave;
And close behind the banner-hidden corse
All draped in black, walks mournfully his horse;
While tears of sound drip through the sunlit day.
A soldier may not weep, but drums and bugles may.

XXXV.
Now, Muse, recount, how after long delays
And dangerous marches through untrodden ways,
Where cold and hunger on each hour attend,
At last the army gains the journey's end.
An Indian village bursts upon the eye;
Two hundred lodges, sleep-encompassed lie,
There captives moan their anguished prayers through tears,
While in the silent dawn the armied answer nears.

XXXVI.
To snatch two fragile victims from the foe

Nine hundred men have traversed leagues of snow.
Each woe they suffered in a hostile land
The flame of vengeance in their bosoms fanned.
They thirst for slaughter, and the signal wait
To wrest the captives from their horrid fate.
Each warrior's hand upon his rifle falls,
Each savage soldier's heart for awful bloodshed calls.

XXXVII.
And one, in years a youth, in woe a man,
Sad Brewster, scarred by sorrow's blighting ban,
Looks, panting, where his captive sister sleeps,
And o'er his face the shade of murder creeps.
His nostrils quiver like a hungry beast
Who scents anear the bloody carnal feast.
He longs to leap down in that slumbering vale
And leave no foe alive to tell the awful tale.

XXXVIII.
Not so, calm Custer. Sick of gory strife,
He hopes for rescue with no loss of life;
And plans that bloodless battle of the plains
Where reasoning mind outwits mere savage brains.
The sullen soldiers follow where he leads;
No gun is emptied, and no foeman bleeds.
Fierce for the fight and eager for the fray
They look upon their Chief in undisguised dismay.

XXXIX.
He hears the murmur of their discontent,
But sneers can never change a strong mind's bent.
He knows his purpose and he does not swerve,
And with a quiet mien and steady nerve
He meets dark looks where'er his steps may go,
And silence that is bruising as a blow,
Where late were smiles and words of ardent praise.
So pass the lagging weeks of wearying delays.

XL.
Inaction is not always what it seems,
And Custer's mind with plan and project teems.
Fixed in his peaceful purpose he abides
With none takes counsel and in none confides;

But slowly weaves about the foe a net
Which leaves them wholly at his mercy, yet
He strikes no fateful blow; he takes no life,
And holds in check his men, who pant for bloody strife.

XLI.
Intrepid warrior and skilled diplomate,
In his strong hands he holds the red man's fate.
The craftiest plot he checks with counterplot,
Till tribe by tribe the tricky foe is brought
To fear his vengeance and to know his power
As man's fixed gaze will make a wild beast cower,
So these crude souls feel that unflinching will
Which draws them by its force, yet does not deign to kill.

XLII.
And one by one the hostile Indians send
Their chiefs to seek a peaceful treaty's end.
Great councils follow; skill with cunning copes
And conquers it; and Custer sees his hopes
So long delayed, like stars storm hidden, rise
To radiate with splendor all his skies.
The stubborn Cheyennes, cowed at last by fear,
Leading the captive pair, o'er spring-touched hills appear.

XLIII.
With breath suspended, now the whole command
Waits the approach of that equestrian band.
Nearer it comes, still nearer, then a cry,
Half sob, half shriek, goes piercing God's blue sky,
And Brewster, like a nimble-footed doe,
Or like an arrow hurrying from a bow,
Shoots swiftly through the intervening space
And that lost sister clasps, in sorrowing love's embrace.

XLIV.
And men who leaned o'er Hamilton's rude bier
And saw his dead dear face without a tear,
Strong souls who early learned the manly art
Of keeping from the eye what's in the heart,
Soldiers who look unmoved on death's pale brow,
Avert their eyes, to hide their moisture now.
The briny flood forced back from shores of woe,

Needs but to touch the strands of joy to overflow.

XLV.
About the captives welcoming warriors crowd,
All eyes are wet, and Brewster sobs aloud.
Alas, the ravage wrought by toil and woe
On faces that were fair twelve moons ago.
Bronzed by exposure to the heat and cold,
Still young in years, yet prematurely old,
By insults humbled and by labor worn,
They stand in youth's bright hour, of all youth's graces shorn.

XLVI.
A scanty garment rudely made of sacks
Hangs from their loins; bright blankets drape their backs;
About their necks are twisted tangled strings
Of gaudy beads, while tinkling wire and rings
Of yellow brass on wrists and fingers glow.
Thus, to assuage the anger of the foe
The cunning Indians decked the captive pair
Who in one year have known a lifetime of despair.

XLVII.
But love can resurrect from sorrow's tomb
The vanished beauty and the faded bloom,
As sunlight lifts the bruised flower from the sod,
Can lift crushed hearts to hope, for love is God.
Already now in freedom's glad release
The hunted look of fear gives place to peace,
And in their eyes at thought of home appears
That rainbow light of joy which brightest shines through tears.

XLVIII.
About the leader thick the warriors crowd;
Late loud in censure, now in praises loud,
They laud the tactics, and the skill extol
Which gained a bloodless yet a glorious goal.
Alone and lonely in the path of right
Full many a brave soul walks. When gods requite
And crown his actions as their worth demands,
Among admiring throngs the hero always stands.

XLIX.
Back to the East the valorous squadrons sweep;
The earth, arousing from her long, cold sleep,
Throws from her breast the coverlet of snow,
Revealing Spring's soft charms which lie below.
Suppressed emotions in each heart arise,
The wooer wakens and the warrior dies.
The bird of prey is vanquished by the dove,
And thoughts of bloody strife give place to thoughts of love.

L.
The mighty plains, devoid of whispering trees,
Guard well the secrets of departed seas.
Where once great tides swept by with ebb and flow
The scorching sun looks down in tearless woe.
And fierce tornadoes in ungoverned pain
Mourn still the loss of that mysterious main.
Across this ocean bed the soldiers fly
Home is the gleaming goal that lures each eager eye.

LI.
Like some elixir which the gods prepare,
They drink the viewless tonic of the air,
Sweet with the breath of startled antelopes
Which speed before them over swelling slopes.
Now like a serpent writhing o'er the moor,
The column curves and makes a slight detour,
As Custer leads a thousand men away
To save a ground bird's nest which in the footpath lay.

LII.
Mile following mile, against the leaning skies
Far off they see a dull dark cloud arise.
The hunter's instinct in each heart is stirred,
Beholding there in one stupendous herd
A hundred thousand buffaloes. Oh great
Unwieldy proof of Nature's cruder state,
Rough remnant of a prehistoric day,
Thou, with the red man, too, must shortly pass away.

LIII.
Upon those spreading plains is there not room
For man and bison, that he seals its doom?

What pleasure lies and what seductive charm
In slaying with no purpose but to harm?
Alas, that man, unable to create,
Should thirst forever to exterminate,
And in destruction find his fiercest joy.
The gods alone create, gods only should destroy.

LIV.
The flying hosts a straggling bull pursue;
Unerring aim, the skillful Custer drew.
The wounded beast turns madly in despair
And man and horse are lifted high in air.
The conscious steed needs not the guiding rein;
Back with a bound and one quick cry of pain
He springs, and halts, well knowing where must fall
In that protected frame, the sure death dealing ball.

LV.
With minds intent upon the morrow's feast,
The men surround the carcass of the beast.
Rolled on his back, he lies with lolling tongue,
Soon to the saddle savory steaks are hung.
And from his mighty head, great tufts of hair
Are cut as trophies for some lady fair.
To vultures then they leave the torn remains
Of what an hour ago was monarch of the plains.

LVI.
Far off, two bulls in jealous war engage,
Their blood-shot eye balls roll in furious rage;
With maddened hoofs they mutilate the ground
And loud their angry bellowings resound;
With shaggy heads bent low they plunge and roar,
Till both broad bellies drip with purple gore.
Meanwhile, the heifer, whom the twain desire,
Stands browsing near the pair, indifferent to their ire.

LVII.
At last she lifts her lazy head and heeds
The clattering hoofs of swift advancing steeds.
Off to the herd with cumb'rous gait she runs
And leaves the bulls to face the threatening guns.
No more for them the free life of the plains,

Its mating pleasures and its warring pains.
Their quivering flesh shall feed unnumbered foes,
Their tufted tails adorn the soldiers' saddle bows.

LVIII.
Now into camp the conquering hosts advance;
On burnished arms the brilliant sunbeams glance.
Brave Custer leads, blonde as the gods of old;
Back from his brow blow clustering locks of gold,
And, like a jewel in a brook, there lies,
Far in the depths of his blue guarded eyes,
The thought of one whose smiling lips up-curled,
Mean more of joy to him than plaudits of the world.

LIX.
The troops in columns of platoons appear
Close to the leader following. Ah, here
The poetry of war is fully seen,
Its prose forgotten; as against the green
Of Mother Nature, uniformed in blue,
The soldiers pass for Sheridan's review.
The motion-music of the moving throng,
Is like a silent tune, set to a wordless song.

LX.
The guides and trailers, weird in war's array,
Precede the troops along the grassy way.
They chant wild songs, and with loud noise and stress,
In savage manner savage joy express.
The Indian captives, blanketed in red,
On ponies mounted, by the scouts are led.
Like sumach bushes, etched on evening skies,
Against the blue-clad troops, this patch of color lies.

LXI.
High o'er the scene vast music billows bound,
And all the air is liquid with the sound
Of those invisible compelling waves.
Perchance they reach the low and lonely graves
Where sleep brave Elliott and Hamilton,
And whisper there the tale of victory won;
Or do the souls of soldiers tried and true
Come at the bugle call, and march in grand review?

LXII.

The pleased Commander watches in surprise
This splendid pageant surge before his eyes.
Not in those mighty battle days of old
Did scenes like this upon his sight unfold.
But now it passes. Drums and bugles cease
To dash war billows on the shores of Peace.
The victors smile on fair broad bosomed Sleep
While in her soothing arms, the vanquished cease to weep.

BOOK THIRD

I.

As in the long dead days marauding hosts
Of Indians came from far Siberian coasts,
And drove the peaceful Aztecs from their grounds,
Despoiled their homes (but left their tell-tale mounds),
So has the white man with the Indians done.
Now with their backs against the setting sun
The remnants of a dying nation stand
And view the lost domain, once their beloved land.

II.

Upon the vast Atlantic's leagues of shore
The happy red man's tent is seen no more;
And from the deep blue lakes which mirror heaven
His bounding bark canoe was long since driven.
The mighty woods, those temples where his God
Spoke to his soul, are leveled to the sod;
And in their place tall church spires point above,
While priests proclaim the law of Christ, the King of Love.

III.

The avaricious and encroaching rail
Seized the wide fields which knew the Indian's trail.
Back to the reservations in the West
The native owners of the land were pressed,
And selfish cities, harbingers of want,
Shut from their vision each accustomed haunt.
Yet hungry Progress, never satisfied,
Gazed on the western plains, and gazing, longed and sighed.

IV.
As some strange bullock in a pasture field
Compels the herds to fear him, and to yield
The juicy grass plots and the cooling shade
Until, despite their greater strength, afraid,
They huddle in some corner spot and cower
Before the monarch's all controlling power,
So has the white man driven from its place
By his aggressive greed, Columbia's native race.

V.
Yet when the bull pursues the herds at bay,
Incensed they turn, and dare dispute his sway.
And so the Indians turned, when men forgot
Their sacred word, and trespassed on the spot.
The lonely little spot of all their lands,
The reservation of the peaceful bands.
But lust for gold all conscience kills in man,
"Gold in the Black Hills, gold!" the cry arose and ran

VI.
From lip to lip, as flames from tree to tree
Leap till the forest is one fiery sea,
And through the country surged that hot unrest
Which thirst for riches wakens in the breast.
In mighty throngs the fortune hunters came,
Despoiled the red man's lands and slew his game,
Broke solemn treaties and defied the law.
And all these ruthless acts the Nation knew and saw.

VII.
Man is the only animal that kills
Just for the wanton love of slaughter; spills
The blood of lesser things to see it flow;
Lures like a friend, to murder like a foe
The trusting bird and beast; and, coward like,
Deals covert blows he dare not boldly strike.
The brutes have finer souls, and only slay
When torn by hunger's pangs, or when to fear a prey.

VIII.
The pale-faced hunter, insolent and bold,

Pursued the bison while he sought for gold.
And on the hungry red man's own domains
He left the rotting and unused remains
To foul with sickening stench each passing wind
And rouse the demon in the savage mind,
Save in the heart where virtues dominate
Injustice always breeds its natural offspring; hate.

IX.
The chieftain of the Sioux, great Sitting Bull,
Mused o'er their wrongs, and felt his heart swell full
Of bitter vengeance. Torn with hate's unrest
He called a council and his braves addressed.
"From fair Wisconsin's shimmering lakes of blue
Long years ago the white man drove the Sioux.
Made bold by conquest, and inflamed by greed,
He still pursues our tribes, and still our ranks recede.

X.
"Fair are the White Chief's promises and words,
But dark his deeds who robs us of our herds.
He talks of treaties, asks the right to buy,
Then takes by force, not waiting our reply.
He grants us lands for pastures and abodes
To devastate them by his iron roads.
But now from happy Spirit Lands, a friend
Draws near the hunted Sioux, to strengthen and defend.

XI.
"While walking in the fields I saw a star;
Unconsciously I followed it afar
It led me on to valleys filled with light,
Where danced our noble chieftains slain in fight.
Black Kettle, first of all that host I knew,
He whom the strong armed Custer foully slew.
And then a spirit took me by the hand,
The Great Messiah King who comes to free the land.

XII.
"Suns were his eyes, a speaking tear his voice,
Whose rainbow sounds made listening hearts rejoice
And thus he spake: 'The red man's hour draws near
When all his lost domains shall reappear.

The elk, the deer, the bounding antelope,
Shall here return to grace each grassy slope.'
He waved his hand above the fields, and lo!
Down through the valleys came a herd of buffalo.

XIII.
"The wondrous vision vanished, but I knew
That Sitting Bull must make the promise true.
Great Spirits plan what mortal man achieves,
The hand works magic when the heart believes.
Arouse, ye braves! let not the foe advance.
Arm for the battle and begin the dance
The sacred dance in honor of our slain,
Who will return to earth, ere many moons shall wane."

XIV.
Thus Sitting Bull, the chief of wily knaves,
Worked on the superstitions of his braves.
Mixed truth with lies, and stirred to mad unrest
The warlike instinct in each savage breast.
A curious product of unhappy times,
The natural offspring of unnumbered crimes,
He used low cunning and dramatic arts
To startle and surprise those crude untutored hearts.

XV.
Out from the lodges pour a motley throng,
Slow measures chanting of a dirge-like song.
In one great circle dizzily they swing,
A squaw and chief alternate in the ring.
Coarse raven locks stream over robes of white,
Their deep set orbs emit a lurid light,
And as through pine trees moan the winds refrains,
So swells and dies away, the ghostly graveyard strains.

XVI.
Like worded wine is music to the ear,
And long-indulged makes mad the hearts that hear.
The dancers, drunken with the monotone
Of oft repeated notes, now shriek and groan
And pierce their ruddy flesh with sharpened spears;
Still more excited when the blood appears,
With warlike yells, high in the air they bound,

Then in a deathlike trance fall prostrate on the ground.

XVII.
They wake to tell weird stories of the dead,
While fresh performers to the ring are led.
The sacred nature of the dance is lost,
War is their cry, red war, at any cost.
Insane for blood they wait for no command,
But plunge marauding through the frightened land.
Their demon hearts on devils' pleasures bent,
For each new foe surprised, new torturing deaths invent.

XVIII.
Staked to the earth one helpless creature lies,
Flames at his feet and splinters in his eyes.
Another groans with coals upon his breast,
While 'round the pyre the Indians dance and jest.
A crying child is brained upon a tree,
The swooning mother saved from death, to be
The slave and plaything of a filthy knave,
Whose sins would startle hell, whose clay defile a grave.

XIX.
Their cause was right, their methods all were wrong.
Pity and censure both to them belong.
Their woes were many, but their crimes were more.
The soulless Satan holds not in his store
Such awful tortures as the Indians' wrath
Keeps for the hapless victim in his path.
And if the last lone remnants of that race
Were by the white man swept from off the earth's fair face,

XX.
Were every red man slaughtered in a day,
Still would that sacrifice but poorly pay
For one insulted woman captive's woes.
Again great Custer in his strength arose,
More daring, more intrepid than of old.
The passing years had touched and turned to gold
The ever widening aureole of fame
That shone upon his brow, and glorified his name.

XXI.
Wise men make laws, then turn their eyes away,
While fools and knaves ignore them day by day;
And unmolested, fools and knaves at length
Induce long wars which sap a country's strength.
The sloth of leaders, ruling but in name,
Has dragged full many a nation down to shame.
A word unspoken by the rightful lips
Has dyed the land with blood, and blocked the sea with ships.

XXII.
The word withheld, when Indians asked for aid,
Came when the red man started on his raid.
What Justice with a gesture might have done
Was left for noisy war with bellowing gun.
And who save Custer and his gallant men
Could calm the tempest into peace again?
What other hero in the land could hope
With Sitting Bull, the fierce and lawless one to cope?

XXIII.
What other warrior skilled enough to dare
Surprise that human tiger in his lair?
Sure of his strength, unconscious of his fame
Out from the quiet of the camp he came;
And stately as Diana at his side
Elizabeth, his wife and alway bride,
And Margaret, his sister, rode apace;
Love's clinging arms he left to meet death's cold embrace.

XXIV.
As the bright column wound along its course,
The smiling leader turned upon his horse
To gaze with pride on that superb command.
Twelve hundred men, the picked of all the land,
Innured to hardship and made strong by strife
Their lithe limbed bodies breathed of out-door life;
While on their faces, resolute and brave,
Hope stamped its shining seal, although their thoughts were grave.

XXV.
The sad eyed women halted in the dawn,
And waved farewell to dear ones riding on.

The modest mist picked up her robes and ran
Before the Sun god's swift pursuing van.
And suddenly there burst on startled eyes,
The sight of soldiers, marching in the skies;
That phantom host, a phantom Custer led;
Mirage of dire portent, forecasting days ahead.

XXVI.
The soldier's children, flaunting mimic flags,
Played by the roadside, striding sticks for nags.
Their mothers wept, indifferent to the crowd
Who saw their tears and heard them sob aloud.
Old Indian men and squaws crooned forth a rhyme
Sung by their tribes from immemorial time;
And over all the drums' incessant beat
Mixed with the scout's weird rune, and tramp of myriad feet.

XXVII.
So flawless was the union of each part
The mighty column (moved as by one heart)
Pulsed through the air, like some sad song well sung,
Which gives delight, although the soul is wrung.
Farther and fainter to the sight and sound
The beautiful embodied poem wound;
Till like a ribbon, stretched across the land
Seemed the long narrow line of that receding band.

XXVIII.
The lot of those who in the silence wait
Is harder than the fighting soldiers' fate.
Back to the lonely post two women passed,
With unaccustomed sorrow overcast.
Two sad for sighs, too desolate for tears,
The dark forebodings of long widowed years
In preparation for the awful blow
Hung on the door of hope the sable badge of woe.

XXIX.
Unhappy Muse! for thee no song remains,
Save the sad miséréré of the plains.
Yet though defeat, not triumph, ends the tale,
Great victors sometimes are the souls that fail.
All glory lies not in the goals we reach,

But in the lessons which our actions teach.
And he who, conquered, to the end believes
In God and in himself, though vanquished, still achieves.

XXX.
Ah, grand as rash was that last fatal raid
The little group of daring heroes made.
Two hundred and two score intrepid men
Rode out to war; not one came back again.
Like fiends incarnate from the depths of hell
Five thousand foemen rose with deafening yell,
And swept that vale as with a simoon's breath,
But like the gods of old, each martyr met his death.

XXXI.
Like gods they battled and like gods they died.
Hour following hour that little band defied
The hordes of red men swarming o'er the plain,
Till scarce a score stood upright 'mid the slain.
Then in the lull of battle, creeping near,
A scout breathed low in Custer's listening ear:
"Death lies before, dear life remains behind
Mount thy sure-footed steed, and hasten with the wind."

XXXII.
A second's silence. Custer dropped his head,
His lips slow moving as when prayers are said-
Two words he breathed "God and Elizabeth,"
Then shook his long locks in the face of death,
And with a final gesture turned away
To join that fated few who stood at bay.
Ah! deeds like that the Christ in man reveal
Let Fame descend her throne at Custer's shrine to kneel.

XXXIII.
Too late to rescue, but in time to weep,
His tardy comrades came. As if asleep
He lay, so fair, that even hellish hate
Withheld its hand and dared not mutilate.
By fiends who knew not honor, honored still,
He smiled and slept on that far western hill.
Cast down thy lyre, oh Muse! thy song is done!
Let tears complete the tale of him who failed, yet won.

Ella Wheeler Wilcox – A Short Biography

Ella Wheeler was born on 5th November, 1850, on a farm in the village of Johnstown, Rock County, Wisconsin. Her parents, Marcus H. Wheeler and Sarah Pratt Wheeler, already had three children. A year earlier the family had moved from Vermont after Marcus's attempts at show business failed and becoming a farmer was his response. With Ella's birth they moved again. This time further north to Madison.

Ella was a gifted child, writing poetry and novels from an early age. The family was poor but her parents believed in education, and whilst little could be afforded they helped as best they could most usefully with grammar, spelling and vocabulary. Her initial education was at the local district school in the village of Windsor, now re-named in her honour as Ella Wheeler Wilcox School.

During her thirteenth year subscriptions the family had been receiving from the New York Mercury, a popular periodical, ceased. This greatly upset her. Life on the farm was lonely and the magazine had been a source of comfort and information about the big world beyond the farm. The family could not afford its own subscription so Ella had to make other plans.

Her writing ambitions were central to this. She wrote two essays but now had to obtain stamps so she could get her submissions in front of editors. She was corresponding with a young girl, Jean, who was in the freshman class at Madison University. Assuring her friend of future payment she enclosed the letter and essays for the New York Mercury.

By 1866, Jean, at Ella's behest, sent a list of all the monthlies and weeklies on the newsstands and Ella was hard at work saving pennies for postage as she began to mail them en masse with her works. Quickly her family lent their support to help out with her endeavours. Ella's mother especially had always thought her daughter would be the one to find the fame, travel and recognition that she had wanted herself and seeing the efforts Ella was putting in she was only to glad to help.

Soon the house the house was filled with ALL the periodicals. Editors would send magazines, books, pictures, bric-a-brac and tableware in response to Ella's requests and works. Being able to earn these items brought her great satisfaction and honed her skills.

She remembers the period in her autobiography:

"The very first verses I sent for publication were unmercifully "guyed" by my beloved "Mercury." The editor urged me to keep to prose and to avoid any further attempts at rhyme. He said that, while this criticism would wound me temporarily, it would eventually confer a favour on me and the world at large.

"My first check came from Frank Leslie's publishing house. I wrote asking for one of his periodicals to be sent to me in return for three little poems I had composed in one day. In reply came a check for ten dollars, saying I must select which one of some thirteen publications they issued at that time.

This bit of crisp paper opened a perfect floodgate of aspiration, inspiration and ambition for me. I had not thought of earning money so soon. I had expected to obtain only books, magazines and articles of use and beauty from the editor's prize-lists; and I had not supposed verses to be saleable. I wrote them because they came to me, but I expected to be a novelist like Mrs. Southworth and May Agens Fleming in time - that was the goal of my dreams. The check from Leslie was a revelation. I walked, talked, thought and dreamed in verse after that. A day which passed without a poem from my pen I considered lost and misused. Two each day was my idea of industry, and I once achieved eight. They sold, the majority, for three dollars or five dollars each. Sometimes I got ten dollars for a poem, that was always an event. Short love-stories, over which I laboured painfully, as story writing was an acquired habit, also added to my income, bringing me ten or fifteen dollars, and once in a while larger sums, from "Peterson's," "Demorest's," "Harper's Bazaar" and the "Chimney Corner."

Ella was beginning to understand the route to success and had the work ethic and creativity to turn it to her advantage. Ella would write her daily quota of poems and other works and then send them out to editors in the hope of getting them published.

It was also about this time that she also left the Country school. Her record in grammar, spelling, reading had of course been excellent but she had a horror of mathematics preferring to spend as much time as possible in the world of her imagination. Ella's talent and determination was such that by now, after she graduated from High School she was already well known in her state as a young writer.

In this she was encouraged by her mother, who despised her own life and felt herself and her family superior to all her neighbours and was forever impressing on the young teenager that her life would blossom and she would achieve success as a writer.

In 1867 her parents sent her to Madison where she was a junior in the Female College, a part of the University of Wisconsin. Ella wanted to spend all of her time writing and begged to come home. She didn't feel the need for further education and was painfully aware of the difference between her homemade clothes and the dresses of city girl. These and other differences caused her to feel left out and not part of the group. After many requests her parents relented and she was allowed home to continue her writing.

In 1870 she was offered employment at $45 a month to edit the literary department of a publication by the magazine's Milwaukee Editor. She accepted, but the hours and work were not to her liking and after three months the magazine folded and her single experience of working in an office was over. Now she was to be a full time author.

In 1872 she published her first book. It was an unusual step as it was a book of poems entitled 'Drops Of Water: Poems' that were solely about abstinence. Published by the National Temperance society it reflected her views on the evils of alcohol and earned her a $50 fee.

She published further books over the next decade but it wasn't until 1883 and the rather racy, for those times, publication of Poems of Passion that her success moved suddenly forward. It was an immediate and large scale success selling over 60,000 in two years.

That same year was also noteworthy for she was engaged to be married. Robert Wilcox was one of many suitors to the young Ella. He was a silver salesman from Meriden, Connecticut. Although they only met three times before the wedding it was to be the relationship that defined her life and much of her work. They married the following year in 1884.

Her most famous poem, "Solitude", was first published on 25th February, 1883 in an issue of The New York Sun. The inspiration for the poem came as she was travelling to attend the State Governor's inaugural ball in Madison, Wisconsin. Whilst travelling to the celebration she was sitting next to a young woman, dressed in black, who was in obvious distress. Ella comforted her for the whole journey. Recalling the widow's emotional state Ella wrote:

Laugh, and the world laughs with you;
Weep, and you weep alone.
For the sad old earth must borrow its mirth
But has trouble enough of its own

She sent the poem to the Sun and received $5 for her effort. It was collected in the book Poems of Passion shortly after in May 1883.

The newlyweds lived for a short time in Robert's home town of Meriden, Connecticut, before moving to New York City and then to Granite Bay in the Short Beach area of Branford, Connecticut. They built two homes and several cottages on Long Island Sound where they would hold gatherings of their literary and artistic friends.

On May 27, 1887, Ella gave birth to a son. Tragically he was only to survive for a few short hours.

In the early years of their marriage, they both developed an interest in theosophy, New Thought, and spiritualism. As this developed Robert and Ella Wheeler Wilcox promised each other that whoever died first would return and attempt to communicate with the other.

Ella had by now published many books of poetry as well as novels and other writings. Her writing life was filled with success on a national scale. Some volumes were collections based on a theme others on a particular time. Some of her war poetry that centred on the Great War in Europe is quite compelling. As she was never considered literary but rather mass market a lot of her work has not received the recognition that other lesser writers have obtained.

In 1916 after thirty years of marriage Robert Wilcox died. Ella was naturally devastated and desperate. Rather than dissipate her grief seemed to grow ever more intense as the days and weeks went by with no message from him. She journeyed to California to see the Rosicrucian astrologer, Max Heindel, seeking help in her sorrow as to why she had no word from Robert. She writes:

"In talking with Max Heindel, the leader of the Rosicrucian Philosophy in California, he made very clear to me the effect of intense grief. Mr. Heindel assured me that I would come in touch with the spirit of my husband when I learned to control my sorrow. I replied that it seemed strange to me that an omnipotent God could not send a flash of his light into a suffering soul to bring its conviction when most needed. Did you ever stand beside a clear pool of water, asked Mr. Heindel, and see the trees and skies repeated therein? And did you ever cast a stone into that pool and see it clouded and turmoiled, so it gave no reflection? Yet the skies and trees were waiting above to be reflected when the waters grew calm. So God and your husband's spirit wait to show themselves to you when the turbulence of sorrow is quieted".

It seemed good advice. She wrote herself a short affirmative prayer to help calm her inner turmoil and would repeat it to herself over and over:

"I am the living witness: The dead live: And they speak through us and to us: And I am the voice that gives this glorious truth to the suffering world: I am ready, God: I am ready, Christ: I am ready, Robert."

She had already written in 1915 a booklet 'What I Know About New Thought which had sold over 50,000 copies. These and other books on New Thought, together with her expanding efforts to educate a wider audience to the powers of positive thinking, were a great comfort to her.

Ella expresses this unique blend of New Thought, Spiritualism and Reincarnation with these powerful words:

"As we think, act, and live here today, we built the structures of our homes in spirit realms after we leave earth, and we build karma for future lives, thousands of years to come, on this earth or other planets. Life will assume new dignity, and labour new interest for us, when we come to the knowledge that death is but a continuation of life and labour, in higher planes".

Ella fell ill in France in early 1919. It was breast cancer. She was taken initially to England and then back to her home. She died of the cancer on October 31, 1919.

Her final words in her autobiography 'The Worlds and I' were:

"From this mighty storehouse (of God, and the hierarchies of Spiritual Beings) we may gather wisdom and knowledge, and receive light and power, as we pass through this preparatory room of earth, which is only one of the innumerable mansions in our Father's house. Think on these things".

A Concise Bibliography
1872   Drops of water, poems.
1873   Shells.
1876   Maurine.
1883   Poems of Passion.
1886   Mal Moule'e, a novel.
1886   Perdita, and other stories.
1888   The Adventures of Miss Volney.
1888   Poems of Pleasure.
1891   A Double Life.
1891   How Salvator Won, and other recitations.
1892   Was it Suicide?
1892   The Beautiful Land of Nod.
1892   An Erring Woman's Love.

1918   Sonnets of Sorrow and Triumph.
1918   The Worlds and I.
1919   Poems.
1919   Cinema Poems and others.
1919   Hello Boys!

Published Posthumously
1920   Poems of Affection.
1920   Great Thoughts For Each Day's Life.
1924   Collected Poems of Ella Wheeler Wilcox.
1927   Gems from E.W.Wilcox

www.ingramcontent.com/pod-product-compliance
Lightning Source LLC
Chambersburg PA
CBHW060147050426
42448CB00010B/2339